C000125126

NORDIC
COOKBOOK

Discover 77 Recipes for Cooking at
Home Traditional and Modern
Scandinavian Dishes

Adele Tyler

© Copyright 2020 by (Adele Tyler) - All rights reserved.

This document is geared towards providing exact and reliable information in regards to the topic and issue covered. The publication is sold with the idea that the publisher is not required to render accounting, officially permitted, or otherwise, qualified services. If advice is necessary, legal or professional, a practiced individual in the profession should be ordered.

- From a Declaration of Principles which was accepted and approved equally by a Committee of the American Bar Association and a Committee of Publishers and Associations.

It is not legal in any way to reproduce, duplicate, or transmit any part of this document in either electronic means or in printed format. Recording of this publication is strictly prohibited and any storage of this document is not allowed unless with written permission from the publisher. All rights reserved.

The information provided herein is stated to be truthful and consistent, in that any liability, in terms of inattention or otherwise, by any usage or abuse of any policies, processes, or directions contained within is the solitary and utter responsibility of the recipient reader. Under no circumstances will any legal responsibility or blame be held against the publisher for any reparation, damages, or monetary loss due to the information herein, either directly or indirectly.

Respective authors own all copyrights not held by the publisher.

The information herein is offered for informational purposes solely and is universal as so. The presentation of the information is without a contract or any type of guarantee assurance.

The trademarks that are used are without any consent, and the publication of the trademark is without permission or backing by the trademark owner. All trademarks and brands within this book are for clarifying purposes only and are owned by the owners themselves, not affiliated with this document.

CONTENTS

Introduction

Denmark, Sweden, Finland, Norway, and Iceland are part of the Nordic Region, the Greenland, Faroe Islands, and Åland. Denmark is a tiny, heavily populated country, the southernmost of the Nordic countries, making up many islands lined with beautiful beaches. Lakes and trees characterize the extensive Finnish landscape. Finland is also known for smartphones, art, and Moomins. The Volcanic Island of the North Atlantic, Iceland, is known for its hot springs and spectacular scenery. Norway is associated with oil and hills, for many. Its stunning, majestic terrain extends from the beach and peaks in the south to the North Cape's midnight sun across the east's rugged areas.

In the Nordic Countries, the largest nation is also the one with the highest population. Sweden is, for many, associated with the manufacture of high-quality vehicles, iron, and steel. The food of northern Scandinavia and the Sami citizens focuses on the few Arctic and sub-Arctic products, primarily reindeer, salmon, and berries.

The largest Nordic people had such restricted variety of ingredients before contemporary days, especially from the far north. Famines have been going on as early as the 19th century. While the industrial revolution arrived late, dining in the Nordic countries in the modern era has become very multicultural. Many traditional foods are focused on what used to be the diet of poor citizens, such as herring, dried cod, potatoes, and hard bread. Many have gained a certain sophistication and are now viewed as classy enough to be freely eaten by the middle or even upper-class citizens.

In the Nordic countries, picking fruit, picking mushrooms, hunting, and fishing are very popular activities, and the first three are readily accessible to foreigners. Almost anywhere there is suitable land for berry picking, and the right of access permits mushroom and such foraging. Fishing is also freely available, although other lure fishing licenses are often easy to obtain. Noma, perhaps the most popular restaurant in the world, opened in 2003 with the ambition of providing a modern take on the Nordic cuisine. Nordic cuisine has many nutritional benefits, as well.

"Nordic Cookbook" has five chapters with an introduction and some delicious Nordic recipes. Chapter one will convey the history of Nordic countries and Vikings, interesting facts about Nordic cuisine, nutritional information, and preparing Nordic food at home. Chapter two is about Swedish traditional and Fika recipes. Chapter three and four will cover Danish and Iceland recipes. In the last chapter, ancient Viking recipes are described to make you enjoy the ancient Nordic foods. Explore more about Nordic cuisine by reading this book now.

Chapter 1: Introduction to Nordic Cuisine

Because of its nutritional advantages, the Nordic diet is contrasted with the Mediterranean diet. According to outlets like Authority Nutrition, it contains less glucose, less salt, half the fiber, and double the fish and seafood relative to a normal Western diet. Some berries have been shown to possess high amounts of omega-3 fatty acids, and cholesterol may be reduced through diets rich in fish oil. Cold-pressed rapeseed is also proven to be as safe as virgin olive oil. To understand more about Nordic food, let's look at history and facts.

1.1 1.1 History of Nordic Foods

Nordic cuisine's heritage depends largely on its Viking background. But the conventional household cooking that provides the basis for the Modern Nordic Cuisine is also present. As oceans cover the Nordic countries, ocean fishing is a large part of these nations' food culture. Whaling in this area is also very high too. Not are whales used for commercial consumption, but they are also consumed in the Nordic countries. An instance of a whale steak came to notice. Scandinavians believe that it could be as delicious as beef if cooked properly.

Other than fish, the most prevalent meal in these countries is frequent catches carried by fishermen. Mostly, salmon and cod are preferred. Pork is the predominant choice when we search for meat on land. Cured, dried, baked, grilled, or roasted, pork is preserved in several ways. Potatoes, fresh spices, beetroot, mushrooms, wild berries, strawberries, imported European fruits like plums, and other imported products are stored, and fruits and vegetables go.

Nordic Cuisine relies more on the ingredients than on sauces. The biggest key is the freshness of the products. The lack of "heavy-butter sauce" in the French style keeps the products' emphasis, as though the ingredients are not great; there is nothing to cover up the poor taste in the dish. When it applies to deserts, a significant proportion of Nordic sweets are pastries. The desserts are strong and very sweet, in addition to the main dishes and many others. To keep the purchaser warm in the winter, they are presumably extremely sweet.

1.2. Vikings Background

The Viking Age was not a time to think about food's fat quality. The Vikings needed all the nutrition that they could get, particularly in winter, in the form of fat. A large part of their diet was beef, fish, fruits, cereals, and dairy products. In the shape of seeds, fruits, and honey, sweet food was eaten. The Vikings were also portrayed as gluttonous in England. According to the Englishmen, they drank and ate so much. The housework needed to be prepared and tailored to the various seasons during the Viking period. A farmer with agricultural animals and crops in the field, the average Viking was self-sufficient. Some people did not develop any of their food and also wanted to purchase it. The blacksmith or fisherman might fulfill his nutritional needs by purchasing or selling goods on the local market.

Every class of civilization, from kings to popular mariners, consumed meat every day was a big advantage of the Viking diet. This may mostly have been pork, as animals were easy to raise and fast to mature, but the Vikings often consumed beef, meat, and livestock.

Horses were also bred for food, a tradition that later led to disputes with Christian officials since, under church belief, horsemeat was a prohibited food.

The Vikings were avid hunters, trapping reindeers, elks, and even bears to get the flames back to the hearth. Although, of course, because the Vikings spent a lot of time on the sea, most of their diet was made up of seafood. Herrings were numerous and prepared in various ways: roasted, salted, grilled, pickled, and even whey preserved.

There were several big drawbacks, considering the overall healthy essence of the Viking diet. From archaeological digs of Viking cesspits and sewer systems, most Vikings struggled from parasites in their digestive tract: they had worms, simply put. The same pulpit excavations showed indigestible seeds consumed by Vikings from all the wheat-baked goods, some of which came from plants that are particularly harmful to humans.

1.3 Interesting Facts

This region of the world is full of seas, rivers, fjords, forestry, and agricultural fields, which have formed the base of the Scandinavian diet over the centuries. You will find that, for example, certain items, such as berries and seafood, are commonly available in the region, mirrored in each nation's dishes. You will also note that a few countries in their diets are very similar-Finland was once a member of Sweden, for instance, so their common dishes are bound to have similarities. Let's look more closely at interesting facts about the Nordic region:

Norway: They are masters of seafood (particularly fish, salmon, and crabs) as described, but you will also see lots of reindeer, lamb, cheese, berries, mushrooms, potatoes cabbage.

Sweden: Lingonberries are certainly a Swedish favorite, and they enjoy their salmon, potatoes, beef, and pork (which you will need for their famed meatballs!) as well.

Iceland: It is no wonder that fish is a big part of the local cuisine covered by ocean, but you will also see plenty of lambs, skyr (yogurt-like), rye flatbread, and berries.

Finland: They enjoy lingonberries, such as the Swedes, yet bilberries, beef, pork, reindeer, mushrooms, salmon, rye bread, and potato are equally common.

Denmark: For the Danes, who enjoy their pork, sausage, rye bread, leafy vegetables, cabbage, salmon, and potatoes, it is typically a hearty diet. Yes, and without a shout at the popular smørrebrød, you cannot even mention Danish cuisine!

Of course, the sweeter stuff in life is enjoyed by all of Scandinavia and the Nordic countries! You will note that they use many kinds of butter, honey, milk, cinnamon, cardamom, and saffron in their sweets, biscuits, and cookies.

.

1.4 Nutrition Facts

The Mediterranean diet is recognized for its correlation with a lower prevalence of chronic diseases such as type 2 diabetes and heart disease. Although there is not enough study on the Nordic diet to make those arguments, the concept is very similar: eat plenty of vegetables, whole grains, legumes, fish, and eat red meat and desserts comfortably. It is not shocking when we start breaking down the Nordic diet to be good for our health. It highlights whole grains that provide nutrition, vitamins, minerals, and nutrients. It is filled with vegetables and fruits that also provide essential nutrients such as vitamins A, C, E, calcium, and fiber. Several small studies have shown that the Nordic diet can help relieve blood pressure. In people with average cognition, the Nordic diet can also help preserve cognition.

1.5 Nordic Food Trends

Here are some of the trends in Nordic cuisine that you need to explore.

Unique and Unconventional Ingredients

Nordic-inspired flavours will modify the whole eating experience. For example, Barnängen can provide you with a sense of Swedish food.

It comprises multiple seeds, spices, and nutritious foods that have been on for a long time in the Swedes.

Fermenting Meat and Sausages

The beef and sausages that are fermented or curated also go perfectly with burgers and hot dogs. You are supposed to have an exciting meaty adventure filled with Nordic salad.

Smoked Food

Nordic countries see foraging as a chance to communicate with the world and to find free food for cooking. The thought of foraging is what most people would enjoy.

Foraging for Food

One of the Nordic cuisine phenomena that you will fall in love with is Smorrebrod. The open sandwich is often synonymous with toast with avocado, although it is unique in the Nordic countries.

Preservation of Produce

There is a special way for the Nordic countries to store their food for the winter months. It is a trend going on for decades, and you can only hope they have mastered the craft by now.

1.6 Essential Ingredients to Prepare at Home

Modern Scandinavian cuisine has been increasingly popular all over the world in recent times. Cloudy hills, open spaces, dense woods with fresh and refreshing air, and clean water define our Nordic scenery. The main ingredients in our Nordic Kitchens are deer, elk, sheep, berries, fruit, and mushroom, as well as seafood of several kinds. One of the key features of modern Scandinavian cooking is elegance. Nordic cuisine is based on fewer ingredients and higher-quality ingredients grown in the hot and dry Nordic climate, which affects the ingredients' taste. While preparing Nordic food at home, you have to collect some basic ingredients that are:

- Apples
- Ramson
- Cloudberries
- Blueberries
- Nordic trout
- Crayfish
- Icelandic skyr
- Mirabelle plum
- Herring
- Erica honey
- Elderflower
- Lamb meat

- Buckthorn berries
- Penny bun mushrooms
- Truffles
- Rye

If a new diet promises to offer supreme health advantages, you do not have to fully revise the eating pattern; if it is rich in fruits, veggies, lean protein, whole grains, and legumes, the Nordic Diet is, then it is sure to be healthy. Without totally exhausting yourself in the phase, your job is to work out how to fit some of your lifestyle values. Know, every day, and your dietary preferences can only eat up a limited portion of your total mental capacity. Step back, take some deep breaths, and try not to overanalyze it if you waste too long debating whether or not to get grain or rye bread.

Chapter 2: Classic Swedish Recipes

Rather than the sweet oats or additionally filling bacon and egg dishes that fill in as the cornerstone of numerous American breakfast menus, Japanese morning meals centre on pungent, appetizing flavours that fulfil and empower you for the afternoon.

The components of this hearty-yet-not-too-filling breakfast might seem more like lunch or dinner to Americans, and that is by design.

2.1 Swedish Meatballs

Cooking Time: 20 minutes

Serving Size: 3 dozen

Ingredients:

- 1 tablespoon lemon juice
- Canned lingonberries
- 1-¾ cups evaporated milk (divided)
- ½ cup of cold water
- 2 teaspoons beef granules
- 1 cup boiling water
- 2 tablespoons flour
- ½ teaspoon allspice
- ¾ cup chopped onion
- 1 pound lean ground beef
- 2 teaspoons butter
- ¼ cup fine dry bread crumbs
- ½ teaspoon salt
- Dash pepper

Method:
1. Apply the dry ingredients to two to three cups of evaporated milk.
2. Remove beef; lightly blend. Until cooled, refrigerate.
3. Form the meat mixture to 1-in with greasy fingers.

4. Heat the butter in a frying pan over medium heat. In quantities, brown meatballs.

5. Use hot water to remove the bouillon. Pour the meatballs over; put them to a boil. Cover; cook for fifteen minutes.

6. In the meantime, stir the cool water and the flour separately.

7. Remove meatballs from the skillet; trim the fat, conserve the liquids.

8. Cook, uncovered, over low heat, swirling until sauce thickens; add flour mixture and remaining evaporated milk to pan juices.

9. Placed the meatballs back in the skillet. Stir in the juice from the lemon.

10. Cover with lingonberries, if needed.

2.2 Old-Fashioned Gingersnaps

Cooking Time: 25 minutes

Serving Size: 4

Ingredients:

- ¼ teaspoon salt
- Additional sugar
- ¾ cup butter (softened)
- 1 teaspoon cloves
- 1 teaspoon ginger
- 2 cups flour
- 1 cup of sugar

- 2 teaspoons baking soda
- 1 teaspoon cinnamon
- 1 large egg
- ¼ cup molasses

Method:

1. Cream the butter and sugar by stirring and mixing in a mug.
2. Whisk in the molasses and egg.
3. Incorporate the flour, baking soda, cinnamon, garlic, salt, and ginger; apply it to the creamed solution. Cool in refrigerator.
4. Flip to 1-1/4-inch. Then dip the balls in sugar.
5. Place 2 inside, apart from ungreased sheets for baking.
6. Bake for about ten minutes at 375 ° or until fixed and the surface cracks. On wire shelves, cool.

2.3 Quick Cream of Mushroom Soup

Cooking Time: 30 minutes

Serving Size: 6

Ingredients:

- 2 cans of chicken broth
- 1 cup half-and-half cream
- 2 tablespoons butter
- ½ teaspoon salt
- ⅛ teaspoon pepper
- ½ pound mushrooms
- 6 tablespoons all-purpose flour
- ¼ cup (chopped) onion

Method:

1. Heat butter over moderate heat in a large frying pan; sauté the mushrooms and onions until soft.

2. Mix the flour, spice, peppers, and 1 can broth until smooth; mix well with the mushroom mixture.

3. Stir the remaining can of broth into it.

4. Carry to a boil; cook and stir for about 2 minutes, until caramelized. Reduce heat; add milk.

5. Simmer, uncovered, until the flavors are combined, about 15 minutes, periodically stirring.

Cooking Time: 30 minutes

Serving Size: 4

Ingredients:

- 3-¾ cups all-purpose flour
- 2 tablespoons butter (melted)
- 1 package active dry yeast
- 2 teaspoons salt
- 2-½cups rye flour
- 1-¾ cups warm water (divided)
- ¼ cup packed brown sugar
- 2 tablespoons shortening
- ¼ cup molasses

Method:

1. Dissolve the yeast in a dish of ¼ of a cup of sugar.
2. Stir well, add butter, molasses, reducing salts and remaining water.
3. Incorporate rye flour; beat until flat. To shape a soft dough, add ample all-purpose flour.
4. Turn to a baking sheet; knead for 6-8 minutes until soft and elastic.
5. Put in a lubricated cup to oil the end, rotating once.
6. Cover and let it rise until doubled, around 1-½ hours, in a hot spot.
7. Shape it into four circular loaves. Place on baking sheets that are greased.

8. Cover and let develop, 45-60 minutes, once doubled.

9. Bake for 30-35 minutes at 350° until lightly browned. Use butter to brush.

2.5 Cheese and Herb Potato Fans

Cooking Time: 75 minutes

Serving Size: 8

Ingredients:

- ½ cup Parmesan cheese (shredded)
- 2 tablespoons chives
- 8 medium potatoes
- ½ teaspoon pepper
- ¾ cup cheddar cheese (shredded)
- ½ cup butter (melted)
- Thyme
- 2 teaspoons salt
- Sage

Method:

1. Preheat the oven to 425 degrees.

2. Trim each potato crosswise into ⅛-inch with a paring blade.

3. Slices, keeping slices connected at the bottom; slightly fan the potatoes and put in a 13x9-in oil dish for baking.

4. Combine the sugar, salt, and black pepper in a shallow saucepan and drizzle over the potatoes.

5. Cook, uncovered, for 50-55 minutes or until soft.

6. Toss the cheese with the herbs in a small bowl; scatter over the potatoes.

7. Bake for 5 more minutes or until the cheese melts.

2.6 Spicy Sticky Cinnamon Rolls with Cream Cheese Icing

Cooking Time: 2 hours and 40 minutes

Serving Size: 24 rolls

Ingredients:

For the Dough

- 1 teaspoon salt
- 4 ½ to 5 cups flour
- 2 ¼ teaspoons dry yeast
- 2 large eggs
- 1 tablespoon vanilla extract
- 1 ¼ cups milk
- 6 tablespoons butter
- ½ cup of sugar

For the Icing

- ½ teaspoon vanilla
- ½ cup milk or cream
- 1 cup powdered sugar
- 4 ounces cream cheese

For the Filling

- 1 cup dark brown sugar
- 1 cup unsalted butter
- 4 cinnamon sticks
- ½ teaspoon cardamom seeds
- 1-star anise pod
- 1 teaspoon coriander seeds

Method:

1. Spray 1½ teaspoon of yeast in the mixing bowl over ¼ cup of lukewarm milk to create the dough and set it aside for five minutes until mildly bubbly.

2. Beat in half a cup of sugar, six tablespoons of melted butter, two big eggs, one teaspoon of vanilla, and one dash of salt using a stick blender's paddle attachment.

3. Stir in the flour, cup at a time, four halves to 5 cups, until the dough is moist and a little sticky.

4. Turn to the dough hooks and knead for five minutes or until the flour clears the blender's side and is firm and smooth in the stick blender.

5. Alternatively, knead for five to six minutes or until soft and stretchy on a floured worktop by hand.

6. Gently coat the dough and bowl with melted butter. Shape the dough into a ball and put it in

a greased bowl, turning it over to ensure that it is oil-coated.

7. Cover with cling film and grow until doubled, around 2 hours, in a warm location.

8. Grind the spices in a spice mixer until perfect for the filling and blend with brown sugar.

9. If you want to miss the extra cloves or use ground cinnamon rather than the whole, swap all the spice with 3 or 4 teaspoons of cinnamon.

10. Soften butter in a blender or with hand beaters along with the spice and sugars.

11. Grease two 9-inch layer pans gently. Roll the dough into a large rectangle on a lightly oiled board, about 14 centimeters by 24 inches.

12. Sprinkle it thickly with the cream sauce butter, and sugar as the dough is spread out, making sure to stretch it almost to the corners.

13. Roll up, stretching and drawing the dough into a taut and strong roll around the long side. To cut it into 24 separate rolls, use a table scraper or knife.

14. Divide the rolls between the prepared plates and let them rise for 45 to 60 minutes in a warm position before the rolls double in size.

15. As the rolls rise, heat the oven to 350F. For 20 to 30 minutes, bake the rolls.

16. Keeping their heat is the easiest way to assess doneness; they are finished around 190 and 200F.

17. Beat the sour cream, milk, syrup, and sugar together for the coating, adding more icing sugar if required to achieve the consistency you want.

18. Drizzle with a fork over the hot rolls. Serve it sweet.

2.7 No-Bake Chocolate Cookies

Cooking Time: 20 minutes

Serving Size: 7

Ingredients:

- 1 tablespoon coffee
- coconut
- 2 tablespoons cocoa powder
- ½ tablespoon vanilla extract
- 1 ½ cups oatmeal
- 6 tablespoons butter
- ¼ cup of sugar

Method:

1. Combine butter, honey, grains, vanilla, cocoa powder, and coffee (remember you never use instant boxes).
2. Roll the length of a meatball into balls.
3. To decorate, roll balls in almond or crystal sugar.
4. Eat right now, or if you want a tougher consistency, refrigerate or freeze.

2.8 Swedish Sticky Chocolate Cake

Cooking Time: 1 hour 45 minutes

Serving Size: 8

Ingredients:

- 1 tablespoon vanilla extract
- ½ cup butter (melted)
- 2 eggs
- 1 ⅓ cups white sugar
- ¼ cup of cocoa powder
- 1 pinch salt
- ½ cup all-purpose flour

Method:

1. Preheat the oven to 300 F degrees Celsius.
2. Grease an 8-inch pie plate gently.
3. Sift the rice, cocoa powder, and salts together; set it aside.
4. Stir the sugars into the eggs until they are smooth.
5. Apply the mixture of flour and whisk only once mixed.
6. Pour in the oil and vanilla extract; stir until well mixed.
7. Pour into a ready-made pie dish.
8. Bake for thirty minutes on the lower rack of the oven or until the middle is partially fixed.
9. Enable the cake to cool on the pie plate for one hour.
10. Serve warm or, nightly, refrigerate, and serve cold.

2.9 Almond Tarts

Cooking Time: 120 minutes

Serving Size: 1 tart

Ingredients:

Dough

- 2 teaspoons whole cardamom
- One small egg
- 7 oz. butter
- ¼ cup of organic cane sugar
- 2 cups flour

Filling

- ½ cup of organic cane sugar
- 3 small eggs
- One cup blanched almond.
- 2.5 oz. butter
- 2 bitter almonds

Icing

- ¼ cup confectioner's sugar
- Juice from an orange

Method:

1. Soften butter, sugar, and eggs together in a big, wide dish. This can be done either in the pan or directly on a clear countertop using your fingertips, mixing in flour.

2. Grind the cardamom as finely as you like with a pestle and mortar.

3. To the dough, apply it and mix properly. For at least 30 minutes, let the dough sit in a cool position.

4. Braise the almonds by dumping boiling water over them and making them sit for a few moments while the pastry mixture rests.

5. When the skin quickly falls off, they are prepared. In a mixing bowl, skin all the nuts and grind them into a good meal.

6. Melt butter in a medium bowl and set aside to cool. In a flexible batter, beat the eggs and the sugars and add the almonds, almond flavoring, and butter.

7. When well mixed, stir together. Grease the little tartlet cartons with butter.

8. With a light coating of dough, line the molds and cover them with the nut mixture nearly to the end.

9. Bake at 400°F in the pan for about fifteen minutes. The cakes are expected to have a light golden color on top.

10. Before extracting the cakes from the mold, let them chill a little.

11. Prepare the icing as the cake bakes. Apply the confectioner's sugar to a little container and drip in the fruit juice.

12. The coating over the tarts should be a little dense but also easy to moisten.

13. Before icing them, wait till the tarts have cooled.

2.10 Chocolate Swiss Roll Cake

Cooking Time: 2 hours

Serving Size: 8 to 10

Ingredients:

For the Cake

- ¼ teaspoon table salt
- 2 tablespoons cocoa powder
- 6 large eggs
- ¾ cup of sugar
- 3 tablespoons strong coffee
- 1 cup of chocolate chips

For the Ganache

- ½ cup heavy cream
- 4 ounces of chocolate chips

For the Filling

- ½ teaspoon vanilla extract
- 2 tablespoons powdered sugar
- 1 cup heavy cream

Method:

1. Heat the oven to 350°F. Butter or grease a jellyroll pan.

2. Cover the bottom with a sheet of waxed or linen paper lengthwise.

3. In a thermal bowl and microwave, mix the chocolate and espresso for 45 seconds.

4. Stir and begin to heat until the chocolate is almost molten, in 2-minute bursts.

5. Continue to stir until it has fully melted. Let it cool.

6. Shake the egg yolks until dark and fluffy in the bowl of an immersion blender fitted with a whisk attachment.

7. Add the sugar steadily and begin to beat until the yolks are light and ribbonry.

8. Stir the cooling chocolate into the egg mix softly.

9. Beat egg whites with salts in a small bowl of an immersion blender fitted with the whisk extension until they maintain stiff peaks.

10. To lighten it up, stir a fifth of the egg white solution into the chocolate yolk mixture.

11. In three combinations, softly incorporate the remaining whites into the cake batter.

12. Drop the batter onto the smooth top of the prepared plate. Bake for 15 minutes in an oven and bake for a jelly roll sheet just until the cake layer is dry to the touch.

13. Switch to a baking sheet and cover the top for ten minutes with a lightly soaked towel.

14. Remove the sheets and loop a knife along the cake's sides.

15. Sift over the top of the cake with one teaspoon of cocoa and protect the cake with a thin coffee or flour sack cloth that is a little longer than the plate.

16. Over the cake, sift the leftover tablespoon of cocoa powder. Roll the cake up with the towel

such that the towel is inside, from short end to short end.

17. Beat heavy cream with powder sugar and vanilla until cold, before stiff peaks are preserved.

18. Have your serve plate ready and put it next to your roll of cake. Unroll the chocolate cake softly.

19. Layer the whipped cream filling thinly over the cake, leaving the far edge with a 1-inch margin.

20. To keep its form, wrap the log securely in plastic and place it in the fridge when cooking the ganache.

21. For 45 seconds, microwave the cocoa and icing in a glass container. Stir and begin to heat until molten and flat, in 20-second bursts.

22. Chill for another ten minutes before it thickens.

23. The cake can be kept for up to two days in the fridge in an airtight bag, but the icing can flatten the longer it is stored.

2.11 Summer Berry Tart

Cooking Time: 50 minutes

Serving Size: 8

Ingredients:

- 1 Vanilla bean seeds
- 1 tablespoon rum

- 600g Mixed berries-
- ½ cup Crème Fraiche
- ¼ cup Icing Sugar
- 4 Meringue nests
- 1 cup Double Cream

For the Tart

- Milk- a little splash
- Butter
- Flour 2 cups
- Unsalted butter 4oz.
- Egg-1 large
- Icing sugar ¼ cup

Method:

1. In a big cup, blend the flour and powdered sugar, add cubed butter and work in the combination until it contains coarse crumbs.

2. Just beat the eggs and a little milk to put the dough together and shape it into a ball.

3. Cover it in plastic wrap and place it for 30 minutes in the refrigerator.

4. Spray some flour with the worktop and the rolling pin, take the mixture out of the refrigerator, and roll it out big enough just to match a 9' loose base tart tin.

5. Lubricate the tart tin with some butter, drain the dough over the rolling pin and pass it to the tart tin to ensure that the sides develop.

6. Trim off the excess bits and stab it all over with a spoon, cover it with a cling film and place it back for 30 minutes in the refrigerator.

7. To 350F, heat the oven.

8. Take out the tart mixture from the refrigerator and line it with baking parchment pressing it to the edges; fill the tart with baked beans or grains and bake it for ten minutes, empty it, remove the baking bean and parchment paper and cook until solid and crispy, allow to cool before lining it for ten minutes longer.

9. Whip the double icing and crème Fraiche with powdered sugar, vanilla bean seeds, and rum until soft peaks are formed before serving.

10.   Combine it with shattered nests of meringue, and the combination will fill your tart.

2.12 Almond cake

Cooking Time: 1 hour 45 minutes

Serving Size: one 9-inch cake

Ingredients:
Cake

- 1 tablespoon orange zest
- 3 tablespoons orange juice

- 3 ½ ounces butter
- ½ cup all-purpose flour
- 3 tablespoons milk
- ¾ cup blanched almonds
- ½ cup brown sugar
- ½ cup natural cane sugar
- 3 egg whites
- 3 egg yolks

Almond and Caramel Topping

- ¾ cup blanched almonds
- ¼ cup brown sugar
- 3 ½ ounces butter

Method:

1. Heat the oven to 175°C.
2. Lubricate a 9-inch springs pan and scatter generously with some breadcrumbs.
3. In a mixing bowl, process the blanched almond for the cake until finely ground; there may still be little bits of almonds remaining.
4. Soften butter and brown sugar together till well mixed and smooth.
5. Insert one egg yolk at a time and blend properly. Sift in the powder and gently fold it into the batter along with the ground almonds.
6. Mix in the orange zest and cream. Stir as little as possible before you have a batter that is even and moist.

7. Mix the egg white in a grease-free cup with an electronic whisk. Add in the cane sugar bit by bit as soft peaks form.

8. Whisk until they form rigid peaks. Fold the combination of sugar and egg white gently into the batter and keep flipping until the batter is mixed uniformly.

9. Onto the greased and breaded spring shape pan, drop the batter. Be alert not to stir unnecessarily.

10. Bake in the lower portion of the oven for 30 minutes at 350°F. When baking a cake, make the almonds and caramel topping fast.

11. Along with the brown sugar, heat the butter. Meanwhile, the majority of the blanched almonds are finely sliced.

12. Add the almonds and mix while the butter and sugar are melted, before the caramel thickness increases.

13. Remove the cake from the oven. Pour the almonds and caramel over, spread it uniformly and carefully.

14. When put into the thickest section of the cake, bake a cake for the next five to ten minutes or until the cake has a good color.

15. Pick the cake and let it cool in the fridge. Remove the cake from the pan until it has cooled.

2.13 Fava Bean and Radish Bruschetta

Cooking Time: 40 minutes

Serving Size: 8

Ingredients:

Cake

- ¼ cup olive oil
- 1 clove garlic (peeled)
- 1 pound fava beans (shelled)
- Black pepper
- 8 baguette slices
- 3 radishes
- 1 tablespoon fennel fronds
- Salt
- 1 teaspoon lemon zest
- 1 tablespoon lemon juice
- 1 tablespoon mint leaves

Method:

1. Hot pan of salted water to a boil and simmer for two minutes with the fava beans.
2. Drain the beans and move them to a big bowl of ice water. Let it cool and rinse, then.
3. Drop off each bean with the outer skin and dispose of the skin.
4. Place the beans in a wide bowl and mash them coarsely, keeping some beans entire or in pieces with a fork.
5. Integrate the fennel fronds, peas, radishes, lime juice, lemon zest, and mint leaves.

6. Sprinkle with salt to taste.

7. Dust olive oil over the baguette slices on both sides and barbecue or broil.

8. Dust the sandwich with cloves, and then place it on top of the fava bean combination.

9. Sprinkle on top with a touch of extra salt and serve.

2.14 Egg, Arugula and Herb Tartine

Cooking Time: 20 minutes

Serving Size: 1

Ingredients:

- 1 egg
- Salt and pepper
- 2 slices good bread
- Several chives stalk
- 1 tablespoon butter
- 1 sprig tender rosemary
- 2 big handfuls of baby arugula

Method:

1. Toast the bread and brush the butter over it.

2. As the remainder of the butter heats in a small strong sauté pan, loosely cut the herbs and arugula.

3. For just less than a minute, or until mildly wilted, sauté the herbs and leaves.

4. Insert the egg and cook rapidly over medium-high heat until the vegetables are barely cooked.

5. Remove away from the heat.

6. Sprinkle with salt, pour on the toasted bread, and eat right away.

2.15 Swedish Ginger Cookies

Cooking Time: 70 minutes

Serving Size: 9 cookies

Ingredients:

- 1 cup of sugar
- 1 large egg (beaten)

- 3 ½ cups all-purpose flour
- 1 teaspoon orange zest
- 1 cup unsalted butter
- 2 teaspoons ginger
- ½ teaspoon salt
- ½ cup dark corn syrup
- 2 teaspoons cloves
- 1 teaspoon baking soda
- 2 teaspoons cinnamon
- Pearl sugar (for dusting)

Method:
1. Whisk together the rice, garlic, cinnamon, ginger, baking soda, and salts in a big cup.
2. Heat the corn syrup and orange zest in a shallow frying pan over medium heat.
3. Insert the sugar and butter and proceed to warm until molten, stirring regularly.
4. Take off from the heat and let it cool down to room temperature. To mix, beat the eggs and combine.
5. To blend, pour over the powder mixture and stir. Shape the dough into a ball, roll it in plastic wrap in the double layer, and chill throughout the night.
6. In the top and bottom thirds of the oven, place the racks and heat it to 375 ° F.
7. Line 2 wide baking sheets parchment paper, with baking paper mats.

8. Roll out a part of the dough on a thinly floured surface to a thickness of ¾ inch using a floured rolling pin.

9. Trim the dough into ideal forms, such as triangles, circles, flowers, rings, gingerbread man, and Christmas trees, using cookie cutters.

10. Bake, turning the cookies between the top and bottom racks and rotating the baking sheets roughly halfway through baking, seven to eight minutes until the edges start to tan.

11. To ensure they do not get too brown, check the cookies closely.

12. Let the cookies cool for five minutes on a cookie sheet before switching to a wire rack to allow them to cool fully.

13. Keep going and slice out the cookie dough's remainder and place the cookies on cooling baking sheets.

2.16 Smoked Salmon Smørrebrød

Cooking Time: 25 minutes

Serving Size: 4

Ingredients:

Horseradish Sour Cream

- Kosher salt

- Ground pepper

- ½ cup (mashed) potatoes

- 1 teaspoon flat-leaf parsley (chopped)
- 1 teaspoon lemon juice
- ½ cup sour cream
- 1 teaspoon dill (chopped)
- 1 tablespoon horseradish

Assembly

- Kosher salt
- Ground pepper
- 4 slices Danish rye
- 2 tablespoons salmon
- Dill sprigs
- 2 radishes (sliced)
- 8 ounces smoked salmon (sliced)

Method:

1. In a shallow cup, whisk together the potatoes, if using sour cream, horseradish, dill, coriander, and lime juice; add salt and pepper.

2. On toast, spread sour horseradish cream and finish with smoked salmon, roe, radishes, dill, and coriander if using.

3. Include spice seasoning.

Chapter 3: Popular Danish Dishes

3.1 Pickled Herring with Danish Rye Bread

Cooking Time: 45 minutes

Serving Size: 4

Ingredients:

- 4 sprigs of thyme
- 2 chilies (crushed)

- 3 shallots
- ½ teaspoon dill seeds
- Half inch piece of ginger
- 1 teaspoon peppercorn
- 1 teaspoon coriander seeds
- 1 teaspoon allspice
- ½ teaspoon mustard seed
- 400 ml of sugar
- 5 bay leaves
- 600 ml vinegar

Method:

1. Start by getting the marinade prepared.
2. In a steel or enamel-coated bowl, gradually warm the vinegar and sugar.
3. When the sugar is fully dissolved, add the other components and leave for approximately 5 minutes over moderate flame.
4. Take the heat from the fermenting marinade and allow it to cool fully.
5. Dust and fillet the herrings, meantime.
6. Cut off the head with a thin, narrow knife and make a puncture in the stomach. Withdraw the insides.
7. Remove the tail and fins off and create a deep cut around the top of the fish.
8. Carefully take one filet off the fish when operating with your fingertips, then softly pull the backbone off the second filet.

9. To slice out bones and trim off extra skin, use a sharp knife.

10. The method of fermenting softens them so that when consumed, they are not visible.

11. Break the fillets into three or four pieces together.

12. Place in the container the herring bits, rotating between surfaces of fish and onions that are pickled.

13. Cover the container with the liquid for pickling.

14. Put a cover on each container and chill in the fridge before eating for at least 12 hours. In the fridge, the pickled herring will last at least two weeks.

15. Using a few fresh basil pieces and a dill sprig to serve 2-3 bits of herring on toasted Danish rye bread.

3.2 Cured Salmon

Cooking Time: 1 hour + freezing time

Serving Size: 4

Ingredients:

- 1 teaspoon of fennel seed
- 1 teaspoon of black pepper
- 2 kg salmon filet
- 1 teaspoon of ground cumin
- 1 teaspoon of mustard seed
- 5 tablespoon sugar

- 2 large bunches of dill (chopped)
- 2 teaspoon coriander seed
- 5 tablespoon coarse salt

Method:

1. Making sure that a very clean glass casserole dish is plenty large to accommodate the filets.
2. Rinse and clean away any scaling with the salmon filets, then pat it dry with a clean cloth.
3. Place the skin side of the filets flat next to one another.
4. Create the remedy by adding the sugar, salt, and seasoning together.
5. Spread uniformly over one of the salmon fillets with the minced dill.
6. Flip over the other fillet and lay it on top of the dill. In the steel casserole, position the stack of fillets and protect them with plastic wrap.
7. To push down on the filets, put a work surface or other flat item on the top filet, and apply a weight of some sort (like a slab).
8. For three days, put it in the fridge the salmon. Flip the fillets every 12 hours over those 3 days.
9. Break the fillets into multiple sections after three days, wrap them in plastic, and freeze for 24 hours.
10. Take out of the freezer and slice thinly when you want to consume your gravad laks by chopping diagonally through the filet.

Cooking Time: 40 minutes

Serving Size: 4 sandwiches

Ingredients:

- 4 slices Danish rye bread
- Lettuce to garnish
- 4 sole fillets
- 1 teaspoon sugar
- Salt to taste
- 4 tablespoon rye flour
- 2 tablespoon pickles (chopped)
- 1 tablespoon lemon juice
- 1 egg
- Butter
- 2 tablespoon parsley (chopped)
- ½ cup crème Fraiche
- 2 tablespoon dill (chopped)

Method:

1. In a cup, blend the crème Fraiche, parsley, dill, lime juice, and honey.
2. To let the flavors come together, put it in the fridge.
3. Whip the egg in a pan.
4. In a cup, add rye flour and season with salt and pepper.

5. Dip the fish fillets in the egg and dredge them with rye flour.

6. Fry pounded fish over medium-high heat in oil until translucent.

7. Remove from the pan and allow it on the paper towel to cool.

8. Cover the lettuce bread with a hot fish filet and a spoonful of sauce.

9. Serve with a slice of lemon and consume with a fork and knife.

10. Enjoy Tuborg with larger wine.

3.4 Danish Liver Paté

Cooking Time: 1 hour 50 minutes

Serving Size: 4-6

Ingredients:

- 6 sprigs thyme
- ¼ teaspoon allspice
- 400g pork (sliced)
- 1 teaspoon salt
- ½ teaspoon pepper
- 1 small white onion, (chopped)
- 4-5 anchovy filets
- 200g pork fat (chopped)
- 2 chicken livers
- 100 ml of milk

- 1 egg
- 1 tablespoon wheat flour
- 200 ml beef broth
- 1 teaspoon butter

Method:

1. Move the liver frequently through the grinding machine using a meat grinder in the finest atmosphere.

2. Grind the pork fat twice, too.

3. To help bind the paté, produce a thickening roux and melt the butter in a small saucepan and add the flour, stir to cover.

4. When boiling, steadily add the broth and then add the cream.

5. Cook softly over medium-low heat until the "batter" is creamy and brown while continuously stirring.

6. Remove from the heat and quit to cool off. Simultaneously, refine the onion, egg, grilled chicken, and seasoning in a food processor or blender until creamy.

7. Incorporate the ground liver, fatty, roux, and mixed components thoroughly.

8. Pour 4-5 tiny aluminum bake pans into the mixture and top each one with a bay leaf.

9. In a wider one, put small baking dishes and fill midway with warm water.

10. Bake for 35-30 minutes in an oven preheated to 350F.

11. Remove the cooked leverpostej and let it cool slightly before using it.

3.5 Tongue Salad

Cooking Time: 25 minutes

Serving Size: 4

Ingredients:

- Juice of 1 lemon
- A pinch of nutmeg
- 1 cup cooked tongue (chopped)
- ½ teaspoon paprika
- 1 egg yolk (boiled)
- 1 tablespoon butter (softened)
- 1 teaspoon Dijon mustard

Instructions:

1. Place the minced tongue aside, and mix all the other ingredients in a large bowl completely.
2. To mix, add the tongues and mix.
3. For extra crunch, serve two spoonful of tongue salads on a piece of buttered Danish rye bread with onions strips! Enjoy it with the knife and fork!

3.6 Brunette Kartofler

Cooking Time: 20 minutes

Serving Size: 4-6

Ingredients:

- 125g sugar

- 8 tablespoons butter (melted)

- 750g small potatoes (cooked)

Instructions:

1. Melt the sugars in a large skillet over medium heat.

2. Leave for several minutes to cook before it becomes golden brown.

3. Stir in the molten butter.

4. Add vegetables. You will have to move them, not so many at a time.

5. Stir constantly until the caramel is uniformly mixed with the potatoes.

6. Place them in a preheated roasting tray and continue until you have finished all the potatoes.

3.7 Fried Pork And Parsley Sauce

Cooking Time: 120 minutes

Serving Size: 4-6

Ingredients:

- Salt

- Pepper

- 1000g pork belly (unsalted)

- 2 dl parsley
- ¼ teaspoon nutmeg
- 1 kg of potatoes
- 4 dl milk
- 1 dl whipping cream
- 50g Danish butter
- 4 tablespoons wheat flour

Instructions:

1. Break the pork belly into slices 5 with a thickness of 6 mm, then dry the cuts for a while on the cling film towel.

2. Before cooking, sprinkle the pieces with salt and black pepper.

3. Begin to peel the potatoes. Place them in a saucepan and cover with cold water.

4. For 15 minutes, steam the potatoes. If you like, you should keep the skin on it. Especially the "new" seasonal potatoes with very small, tender white skin.

5. Cut the parsley into bits. Create a butterball of butter and starch and constantly stir until the combination is turned into a uniform mass when melting in the saucepot.

6. Add the milk and mix. Repeat until you like the sauce with the consistency you want. Not too dense and not too thin.

7. Do not cook the gravy. A kind of white "béchamel sauce" will end up.

8. Stir in the whipped cream, then taste the sauce.

9. Put in nutmeg - if you like. Then insert all the chopped parsley when mixing - and add salt and pepper to taste.

10. Let the sauce boil for ten minutes while soaking up the flavor - so the components are blended and stirred together.

11. On either side of a hot pan, cook the pulled pork sliced for almost two minutes with medium heat until they seem crisp and with a translucent surface.

12. In the heated 200°F oven, place the pork belly and roast for 20 minutes - thus rotating the slices after quarter reheating time.

13. It is easier to barbecue the pork belly strips on a well-heated camping stove in the summertime.

14. Place on a warm surface the lukewarm potato and place the crispy pork belly pieces, then spill over the potato the hot and dry parsley sauce.

15. Toss the dish with some fresh minced parsley and eat.

3.8 Danish Rice Dessert

Cooking Time: 90 minutes

Serving Size: 4

Ingredients:

Rice Pudding

- 1-liter milk
- 2 vanilla beans

- 1 dl water
- 2.25 dl white rice

Risalamande

- 5 dl heavy cream
- One can cherry sauce (for topping)
- 2 tablespoon sugar
- 150 g almonds

Instructions:

1. Transfer the rice and water to a saucepan. Warm it up and let it simmer for two minutes or so.

2. Transfer the milk to the mixture and cook until it boils, stirring continuously.

3. Add the vanilla bean pods. This is accomplished by cutting the vanilla beans by using a knife to scrape out the pods.

4. Use two tablespoons of sugar to incorporate the vanilla. Additionally, add to the mixture the hollow vanilla beans.

5. Let the pudding boil at low temperatures under the cover. The rice continues to burn in the saucepan, so don't forget to stir periodically.

6. For about 35 minutes, let it boil.

7. Take the empty vanilla beans. Now the rice pudding is finished.

8. Before continuing to make the Risalamande, let it chill in the refrigerator. You can prepare this rice pudding the first day in advance.

9. Heat the water and pour it into a shallow saucepan until the boiling point.

10.   For around 5-7 minutes, add the nuts and let them sit in the warm water.

11.   The almonds are picked up one-by-one and squeezed middle finger so that the peel extracts from the almond. When required, add more hot water.

12.   Skinning almonds should be simple. Cut the almonds thinly sliced and blend them with the cool rice pudding.

13.   Add it to the dessert with cold rice and blend properly.

14.   In a separate pan, mix the heavy cream into whipped cream and mix gently with the rice pudding.

15.   The Risalamande has now been completed. On serving, place it in the refrigerator.

3.9 Danish Meatballs

Cooking Time: 65 minutes

Serving Size: 6

Ingredients:

- Salt and pepper to taste
- ¼ cup margarine
- ¼ cup all-purpose flour
- ¼ cup seltzer water
- ½ pound veal
- 1 egg
- ¼ cup bread crumbs
- ½ pound pork
- ¼ cup onion
- ¼ cup milk

Instructions:

1. In a dish, mix all the veal and pork and whisk in the milk, cabbage, and egg.
2. Add the crumbs of the bread to the beef. Sprinkle with the flour and squeeze to mix properly.
3. Stir in the water from the seltzer, sprinkle with salt and black pepper and, blend properly.
4. The blend should be very sticky, but it should not spill.
5. In the fridge, chill the leftover marinade for 30 minutes to make the meatballs easier to mold.
6. Heat the margarine over moderate heat in a large pan.

7. Scoop up roughly 2½ tablespoons of cooking liquid with a large spoon to shape meatballs, and form the combination into a slightly compressed, circular meatball about the size of an average egg.

Put the meatballs into the heated pan, and fry for around fifteen minutes per hand, until the meatballs are well-browned and no longer pink in the middle

3.10 Danish Roast Pork With Cracking

Cooking Time: 105 minutes

Serving Size: 5

Ingredients:

- coarse salt
- 5 dried bay leaves
- 1kg Boneless pork roast

Instructions:

1. To carve long, deep grooves in the crust of the pork roast, use a paring blade.
2. The grooves can have a separation of around 5 mm (half an inch).
3. Make sure that the rind has deep grooves, but do not hack through the real beef.
4. Clean the whole roast with coarse sea salt deeply. Make sure you get a lot of salt from the grooves.
5. In the grooves, position 3-6 dried bay leaf - if you would not have any, this can be skipped.
6. On a shelf with a baking dish underneath, put the roast.

7. Put two cups (half a liter) of water and some diced onions and carrots in the roasting pan. This water will later be used on the veggies to make a good gravy.

8. Be sure that in a normal direction, the roast is sitting. To level it, you should use a ball of aluminum foil beneath the roast.

9. If you are not doing this, you risk having an inconsistent color or burning the rind. Heat the oven to 440 F and let the roast cook for fifteen minutes.

10.   Switch down the temperature to 400 F and begin to cook.

11.   Switch on the grill option in the oven when the temperature is 57C. This means that the rind will be fresh and crisp.

12.   Keep an eye on your roast because you're not going to burn it.

13.   When the temperature is 65C, the roast is cooked at 150 F. To attain this level, and it takes about 50 minutes. You should add a little extra if the water evaporates while cooking.

14.   Take it out of the oven when the roasting is finished. Let it rest for about fifteen minutes or quickly eat it.

15.   Drain the vegetables from the water and dump them into a saucepan if you want to make a good gravy.

16.   Apply some heavy cream and some coloring with brown gravy. To taste, apply salt.

3.11 Danish Cold Buttermilk Soup

Cooking Time: 15 minutes

Serving Size: 5

Ingredients:

- 1 tablespoon sugar
- 1 tablespoon lemon juice
- 2 tablespoon cane sugar
- 1 vanilla bean
- 4 egg yolks
- 1-liter buttermilk
- 1-liter plain yogurt

Instructions:

1. Mix the yolks and sugars into a soft and airy mixture using a hand mixer.

2. From a vanilla bean, pick the vanilla seeds out.

3. Use one tablespoon of sugar to combine the vanilla seeds.

4. Along with the yolks, stir the vanilla bean.

5. Stir the egg yolks with the yogurt. Add four steps of the yogurt and shake well in between each phase.

6. Eventually, add the buttermilk and blend it well. Add lime juice flavoring.

7. Leave the soup in the fridge with the buttermilk.

8. The unused vanilla beans should be left in the cup as they still have a lot of wonderful taste.

3.12 Danish Breaded Pork Patties

Cooking Time: 30 minutes

Serving Size: 2-3

Ingredients:

- Salt and pepper
- 50g of butter
- 2 tablespoon water
- 70g bread crumbs
- 1 egg
- 500g ground pork

Instructions:

1. Begin by splitting the meat into five pieces of approximately 100 g total and turning them into dense circular patties.
2. Beat the egg and the water on a deep pan.
3. Mix the bread crumbs along with pepper and salt on a second pan.
4. Now, in the beaten egg, roll the pork patties and then in the breadcrumbs.
5. Be sure the breadcrumbs surround the whole patty.
6. One time should be adequate, but if you want a thicker breading sheet, repeat this move once again.
7. Transfer the butter to the frying pan and cook the breaded pork patties for around 5 minutes.
8. Switch them over from moment to moment.

3.13 Danish Red Berry Pudding

Cooking Time: 1 hour 15 minutes

Serving Size: 5

Ingredients:

- 2.5 dl water
- 2 tablespoon potato starch
- 125g strawberry
- 125g sugar
- 1 teaspoon vanilla extract
- 125g blackcurrant
- 125g redcurrant
- 125g raspberry

Instructions:

1. When you are using fresh berries, begin by using cold water to rinse and clean them.
2. Cut in on lower rates for raspberries and strawberries.
3. Move all of the ingredients into a frying pan except the potato starch.
4. Mix all the ingredients and let the berries sit for about an hour in the sweet liquid.
5. Use medium-high heat to heat the combination of berry and water until it boils.
6. For eight minutes, let the solution boil.

7. Turn the heat down and add the cornflour that has been dissolved.

8. Let the red berry pudding boil for an extra five minutes, and stop boiling the mixture.

9. Until serving with cold heavy cream, spill the pudding into 3-4 dishes and let it chill off.

10.   Sour cream combined with some vanilla seed is a substitute for heavy cream.

3.14 Danish Apple Cake

Preparation time: 45 minutes

Serving Size: 6-8

Ingredients:

- 300ml whipping cream
- 1 tablespoon plain chocolate
- 500g Brimley apples
- 200g rolled oats
- 125g granulated sugar
- 500g dessert apples
- 2 teaspoon vanilla sugar
- 50g butter
- 3 tablespoon sugar

Instructions:

1. Fill the water in a big jar.

2. Peel, center, and dice the apples thinly and lower them into the water.

3. Drain the water and leave one tablespoon of stewed apples with two tablespoons of sugar and powdered sugar under the cover until tender. (Approximately ten to twenty minutes).

4. Transfer to a bowl of baked apple slices and let settle.

5. Melt the butter over light heat in a large deep fryer, add 125g of sugar, and mix with a spoon.

6. Mix in the grains until they are crispy and buttered once the sugar has turned into caramel with butter (this will take a couple of minutes).

7. (Be careful, so you do not burn). Enable for cooling.

8. Finally, whisk the cream and put half the apple combination in a cup, followed by half the buttered grains, then add a cream layer and customize with rubbed chocolate.

9. Serve right away or until necessary, chill.

3.15 Danish Chicken Tartlet

Cooking Time: 50 minutes

Serving Size: 4

Ingredients:

- 400-gram white asparagus
- Tartlet shells
- 500-gram meat
- 70-gram butter

- 4 tablespoons of flour
- 2 dl Chicken stock
- 2 dl milk
- 1.5-liter water

Instructions:

1. The water should be boiling, and the stock applied.
2. Insert the meat from the hen or poultry and simmer for 20 minutes.
3. Let the chicken over and cut it into tiny chunks, preferably little triangles,
4. Save the fried chicken water.
5. Cook once soft and sliced if fresh asparagus is used.
6. When the butter has melted, take a casserole dish and add butter and starch.
7. Transfer the milk and some boiled chicken water to the mixture.
8. Add a pinch of salt to the sauces and allow for a few minutes to boil.
9. Add the chicken and asparagus to the pan to make sure it is hot.
10. It is time to fill up the tartlets then. Chop parsley and seasoning on top of the tartlets when completed.

3.16 Danish Rye Bread

Cooking Time: 12 hours 25 minutes

Serving Size: 2 bread

Ingredients:

- 1 tablespoon salt
- 2 tablespoon gravy browning
- 2 dl rye kernels
- 4 dl all-purpose flour
- 4 dl rye flour
- 2 dl wheat
- 4 dl sourdough
- 8 dl water
- 2 dl flax seed
- 1 tablespoon malt syrup
- 2 dl sunflower seeds

Instructions:

1. Put the crushed rye kernels, broken wheat, flaxseed, sunflower seeds, water, malt syrup, and sticky dough into a large bucket.

2. Enable all to soak for at least eight hours. This can be achieved in the evenings with benefit so that you can begin the next morning.

3. Insert the remaining ingredients after about eight hours and allow the rye bread dough to rise for about 45 minutes.

4. Cut the mixture into two pieces and dump it into two ordinary pans of bread.

5. With plastic tape, coat the bread pans with.

6. For around 1-2 hours, let the bread rise or the dough pan is full of bread.

7. Bake the rye bread for around 1 hour at 180C.

8. Take the bread from the bread pots and let them cool off until finished.

9. Hold them in an air-tight jar or a plastic bag while the bread is cooled down.

3.17 Danish Meatloaf

Cooking Time: 60 minutes

Serving Size: 4-6

Ingredients:

- Salt and pepper
- 1 pack of bacon
- 1 pound ground pork
- 2 eggs
- 2 tablespoons plain breadcrumbs
- 1 pound ground beef

Sauce

- salt
- milk and all-purpose flour
- 1 cup milk
- a few drops gravy browning
- 2-3 teaspoons redcurrant jelly

Instructions:

1. Sauté the onions and green pepper for five minutes in the butter.

2. Transfer the hot sauce and water to ¼ cup and simmer for another 3 minutes.

3. In a 9x5x3 loaf tray, press the onion mixture onto the rim.

4. Mix the rest of the ingredients and press the onion mixture evenly.

5. Bake for 1 hour at 375°F.

6. Invert the meatloaf on a plate before serving so that the onion/pepper combination is on top.

7. Mix all ingredients of the sauce and cook until thickens. Serve with meatloaf.

Chapter 4: Iceland Food Recipes

4.1 Prawn Paella

Cooking Time: 40 minutes

Serving Size: 4

Ingredients:

- 375g of Iceland king prawns
- 1 tablespoon of Iceland coriander
- 6 bags Iceland golden savory rice
- 1 tablespoon olive oil
- 1 large Iceland onion
- 1 tablespoon Iceland garlic

To Serve

- Lemon wedges

Instructions:

1. In the oil, fry garlic and onion over medium-high heat until they become softer and begin to color. It should be finished in five minutes.
2. Transfer the frozen prawns to the dish and swirl to coat in the mixture until they are nearly defrosted, frying for five minutes, stirring regularly.
3. Add 4-6 sachets of frozen gold rice plus cilantro.
4. To mix, whisk gently.
5. Serve with chopped parsley on the plate.

Cooking Time: 60 minutes

Serving Size: 4

Ingredients:

- About 12 lasagna sheets
- Large handful of mozzarella
- 1 tablespoon olive oil
- Jar of tomato sauce
- Jar of white sauce
- A small handful of Iceland onions
- 1 tablespoon Iceland garlic
- ½ packet of roasted vegetables
- A whole packet of steak mince

To Serve

- Garlic bread
- Salad

Instructions:

1. Heat up to 180C oven.

2. Sauté the garlic and onions in the oil until they soften. Stir in the mince, then fry until browned.

3. Until it's cooked, add vegetables. When you have picky eaters, remove and chop some very big vegetables.

4. Tip into a tomato saucepot, bring to a boil, and cook for 20 minutes.

5. Get the bakery dish and layer it up! Start with a meat sauces layer, then a pasta line (lasagna sheets-use 4-7 in one layer and split up if necessary). There's a layer of cheese sauce now. Then repeat, depending on how large your dishes are, once or several more.

6. Complete the layering with spaghetti, then white sauce, and then apply a generous layer of diced mozzarella to the end. Place it in the oven.

7. When it's heating, pop in your garlic bread at the end and prepare your salad.

8. Bake for 40 minutes until the spaghetti is cooked through and crispy and boiling. Stick a toothpick in the middle to ensure the pasta is good and fluffy all the way around.

9. Serve with salads and toast with garlic

4.3 Beef Enchiladas

Cooking Time: 50 minutes

Serving Size: 4

Ingredients:

- 1 tablespoon chili (chopped)
- Drizzle extra virgin olive oil
- 8 soft tortillas
- 2 large handfuls of cheddar
- 1 tin tomatoes
- 1 tablespoon frozen coriander (chopped)
- 1 tablespoon olive oil
- A small handful of frozen onions (chopped)
- 1 packet of chili spice mix

- 1 jar of kidney beans
- 1 tablespoon frozen garlic (chopped)
- ½ packet of mixed peppers (sliced)
- A whole packet of beef mince

To Serve
- 1 tablespoon chili
- Side salad
- A handful of avocado chunks
- 1 tablespoon of coriander
- Dollops sour cream

Instructions:

1. Defrost the avocado several hours in advance.
2. Heat the oven to 180C.
3. Sauté the garlic and onions in the oil until soft. Stir in the mince and simmer until it's colored.
4. Top in the pepper and seasoning blend and stir constantly.
5. Soak beans, tinned toms, and cilantro now tap in. Let it boil gently with the lid off for 20 minutes.
6. Find a huge baking dish and a breadboard.
7. Place 1 wrapper on the board and spoon down the center of the meat combination.
8. Wrap it and pass it to the baking bowl, making sure it is beneath the tucked in a bit to not unravel. For seven more, do the same.
9. Over the end, grate tons of cheddar and scatter chili on too. Drizzle some extra virgin olive oil with it.

10.　　　Pop it in the oven and simmer for 25 minutes.

11.　　　Make your guacamole by just thoroughly mixing your avocado with cilantro, chili, and coriander.

12.　　　Serve with a spoonful of sour cream, guacamole, and lettuce (or creme fraiche dip).

4.4 Fish Finger Pie

Cooking Time: 25 minutes

Serving Size: 4

Ingredients:

- 1 packet of mashed potato
- Large handful mild cheddar
- 2 tins of baked beans
- 10 fish fingers

To Serve

- 1 packet of tender stem broccoli

Instructions:

1. Heat the oven to 180C.
2. Get a squared dish for baking. Pour the beans down. Lay on top of the fish fingers.
3. For three minutes, microwave your mix.
4. For another two minutes, mix and prepare.
5. To the sandwich, add a coat of mash and sprinkle on tons of grated cheese.
6. For 20 minutes, roast.

7. For three minutes, boil the broccoli. Mix and serve.

8. Try to transfer a spoonful of curry powder or Barbecue sauce to the beans.

4.5 Kuromame Sweetened Black Soybean

Cooking Time: 30 minutes

Serving Size: 4

Ingredients:

- ½ iceberg lettuce
- 4 burger buns
- 4 mini chicken fillets
- 4 tablespoon mayonnaise
- ½ jar pesto

Options to Stack

- 2 tomatoes (sliced)
- 4 Onion rings
- 4 Hash browns

To Serve

- Iceland Corn on the cob
- Iceland sweet potato fries

Instructions:

1. Remove across all packages 4 mini chicken fillets, put on a plate with plastic wrap.

2. Defrost for 13 hours in a freezer.

3. Preheat the oven to 200C.

4. Pop in your 20-minute hash browns and potato wedges, then four minutes later, your onion rings for 16 minutes. Keep an eye on the one minute earlier.

5. In a bowl, ferment the pesto and mix the chicken fillets with pesto to coat them.

6. In a saucepan, heat the oil until warm and fry the fillets for about fifteen minutes, rotating once. Pop the corn for five minutes on the cob in the microwave.

7. Get each burger bun divided. Pop it under the barbecue or in the toaster.

8. Take out the buns and drench the bottom with a touch of extra pesto.

9. Insert the chicken breast, a little chopped lettuce, and then drop some mayo into the top piece. Then pop it on, or line it up.

10. To end, pop a brown hash underneath the chicken, an onion ring on top of the salad, and then a sliced tomato.

11. Serve on the corn with sweet potato chips and corn.

4.6 Superboost Smoothie

Cooking Time: 3 minutes

Serving Size: 4

Ingredients:

- Splash orange juice
- Splash water
- Handful of strawberry
- Handful spinach
- Handful banana

Instructions:

1. Put in a handful of mixed berries and bananas.
2. Put a couple of spinach nuggets.
3. Drop a shot of juice and transfer water to the top.
4. To beautify, reserve a few strawberries.

4.7 Beef Chili Nachos

Cooking Time: 10 minutes

Serving Size: 12

Ingredients:

- Handfuls cheddar cheese
- Handful of avocados
- 1 tablespoon olive oil
- 1 tin of kidney beans
- Tortilla chips
- 475g bag steak mince
- 1 handful onions
- 1 stock cube

- 1 tin tomatoes
- 1 tablespoon garlic
- 1 packet of chili mix con Carne
- 1 teaspoon chili

To Serve

- Dollops of sour cream dip

Instructions:

1. In the butter, fry the onions and garlic for five minutes or until softened.
2. Insert the mince and fry until it is no longer frozen. It could take 5 to 10 more minutes.
3. For the last couple of minutes, top in the stock cube plus the spice mixture.
4. Transfer tanned tomatoes and soaked kidney beans.
5. Turn the heat on and cook with no cover for fifteen minutes, causing most of the liquid to disappear.
6. Now put some tortilla chips on a cookie dish or wide baking sheet, then blot mouthful of the beef chili plus the sauce, the preserved avocado, some cheese and then replicate again: a coating of tortilla chips, then dot over the beef pepper, hot sauce, avocado, and loads of cheese.
7. Pop it for fifteen min under a hot pan. Keep an eye out, as this will capture you quickly.
8. Offer with spoonful of sour cream dip at the center of the table and encourage others.

9. If you like this super spicy, at the vegetables and garlic level, simply add a lot more frozen pepper to the combination.

3.8 Berry Crumble

Cooking Time: 30 minutes

Serving Size: 4

Ingredients:

- 100g plain flour
- 4 tablespoon sugar
- 1 tablespoon brown sugar
- 50g cold butter cubes
- 1 bag of berries

Instructions:

1. Preheat the oven to 180C. Add a spoonful of sugar to combine.
2. Scatter frozen fruit into a cookie sheet.
3. Rub the starch into the butter until it feels like breadcrumbs, and lightly rub.
4. Mix in the sugar now.
5. Cover the fruit with a sprinkle topping.
6. Spray a little additional sugar on top and bake for about thirty minutes or until the fruit is bubbling and it's baked through and caramelized on top.
7. With custard or milk, prepare.
8. Try this in the mixture of sliced apples, too. Orbits of rhubarb.

4.9 Super Veg Cottage Pie

Cooking Time: 60 minutes

Serving Size: 4

Ingredients:

- 1 packet of carrot and mash sweet potato
- Handful of cheddar
- 1 tablespoon olive oil
- 1 beef stock cube
- A handful of mixed vegetables
- 1 tin of tomatoes
- 1 tablespoon of mixed herbs
- Whole packet beef mince
- Small handful onions
- 1 tablespoon garlic

Serve

- Cabbage
- Gravy

Instructions:

1. Heat the oven to 180C.
2. Sauté in oil with onions and garlic. Insert beef mince when defrosted and fry until golden.
3. Insert the vegetables and whisk until the mixture is defrosted.
4. Now add the bucket of stock, the fresh basil, and the tomatoes.

5. Bring it to a boil and cook for 20 minutes.

6. As per packet directions, microwave your carrot mash and sweet potato.

7. In a baking bowl, pop the beef mixture and cover it with the mash.

8. Insert lots of cheese and cook until crispy and bubbling, for 30-40 minutes.

9. Tear a cabbage and pour some hot water over it for ten minutes until it is supposed to come out and cook with a cover.

10. Toss in the sugar, salt, and black pepper, then rinse. Make the gravy.

11. Serve the gravy and vegetable pie.

4.10 Superboost Soup

Cooking Time: 40 minutes

Serving Size: 4

Ingredients:

- 1 stockpot
- 1 tablespoon coriander
- ⅔ bag floret and carrot mix
- ¼ bag frozen spinach
- 1 teaspoon ginger
- 1 teaspoon chili
- 1 tablespoon olive oil
- 1 tablespoon garlic
- Handful onions

Instructions:

1. Sauté in oil with onions, garlic, chili, and spice.

2. To cover the vegetables, add floret and carrot mixture and ample made-up stocks.

3. Simmer until it becomes soft. Near the top, insert spinach for about ten minutes before it splits and can be blended in.

4. Whizz the soup until creamy and nice. If required, include a little boiling water to release it.

5. Right into the spicy broth, add cilantro.

6. Do not add too many stocks in because it is much harder to soften if you bring in too much.

7. When using beef stock or bowls, don't sprinkle with salt as they are always salty.

4.11 Beefy Baked Bean Pie

Cooking Time: 45 minutes

Serving Size: 4

Ingredients:

- Iceland frozen mash

- Grated Iceland mild cheddar

- 1 tablespoon olive oil

- 1 beef stock cube

- A little pepper
- Small handful onions
- 2 tins of baked beans
- A whole packet of beef mince

To Serve

- Jug of gravy
- Iceland petit poi's

Instructions:

1. Heat the oven to 180C.
2. In the butter, soften the onions.
3. In the grill, add the meat and defrost, and cook until golden.
4. Insert a stock cube and a bit of water (half of the total of a mug) and get it to boil.
5. Carry the beans to 2 tins. Take it to a boil and cook for fifteen minutes.
6. With some spice, season.
7. Microwave the pie with enough mash to coat it.
8. Pour it into a bowl for cooking.
9. Cover with mash and a lot of grated cheese afterward. For 20 minutes, roast.
10. Serve with the beans and a mug of gravy made and use the box instructions.
11. Try this in place of mince or sausages. Simply cook the frozen sausage rolls for 15 minutes and cut the onions and garlic.

4.12 Tasty Chicken Curry

Cooking Time: 50 minutes

Serving Size: 4

Ingredients:

- 1 handful of spinach
- 1 handful of fine green beans
- 1 tablespoon vegetable oil
- 1 jar of mild curry sauce
- A small handful of coriander
- Small handful onions
- 1 tablespoon chili
- ½ a packet of mini chicken fillets
- 1 tablespoon garlic
- 1 tablespoon ginger

To Serve

- 2 packets of Plain naan bread
- 4 bags of white rice

Instructions:

1. In oil, cook the onion, ginger, garlic, and chili.
2. Insert the mini chicken fillets and fry until nearly cooked and no more frozen.
3. Chop them in two with a set of clean blades if you find them too big for your family.
4. Insert the curry sauce, put it to a boil, and cook for fifteen minutes.

5. Include the spinach after four minutes. Stir to melt when it defrosts.

6. Seven minutes until you are about to eat, add cilantro and green beans. Occasionally swirl.

7. In the oven, cook the naan bun and heat the rice.

8. Whatever you want, add extra chili. Get it colder by choosing a cooler sauce container.

4.13 Secret Ingredient Chocolate Cake

Cooking Time: 40 minutes

Serving Size: 4+

Ingredients:

- 1 teaspoon baking powder
- 1 large egg
- 150g dark chocolate
- 900g ¼ bag of mashed potato
- 100g sugar
- 200g self-rising flour
- 100g condensed milk

Milk Chocolate Icing

- 20g block butter
- 150g condensed milk
- 150g milk chocolate

Instructions:

1. The night ahead, defrost the mash in the freezer.

2. Heat the oven to 180C.

3. Over a pan of boiling water, pop a heatproof mug. Do not let the water hit the bowl.

4. Melt the broken bar of chocolate in a pan. Insert condensed milk, butter, and sugar. Gently blend as it is melting.

5. Remove from the heat and enable to cool down slightly.

6. In a pan, season the flour and mixing powder, transfer the mash to the pot, and mix the chocolate combination.

7. Shake and add the egg, too. Mix thoroughly.

8. Grease and cover with greaseproof paper 20cm loosely bottom sandwich muffin tins.

9. Transfer the blend to the tins, separating evenly.

10. Roast it for thirty minutes. Do the icing in the meantime.

11. Like the above, melt the cookies, condensed butter, and milk. Just allow it to cool.

12. Enable the cakes in their tins to cool slowly, then extract them from the tins and enable them to cool entirely.

13. For the coloring, sandwich the cakes together. Then top this all over the edges with some too-smother.

14. Customize the buttons with cocoa powder.

4.14 Cheat's Berry Brulee

Cooking Time: 15 minutes

Serving Size: 4

Ingredients:

- 1 pack of custard
- Brown sugar on top
- 2 tablespoon sugar
- Half a pack of different berries

Instructions:

1. To make a puree, boil the frozen fruit with two tablespoons of sugar.
2. Fill four heatproof compote saucepans with ¾ of them.
3. As directed, heat the custard in the microwave.
4. Put a nice sprinkle of brown sugar on top and load each ramekin with hot custard.
5. Pop it under a hot pan until it fills with honey.
6. A blow torch is an ideal way for the same result to be done! But if you do not have one, it is just fine with the grill.

4.15 Sunday Roast

Cooking Time: 90 minutes

Serving Size: 4

Ingredients:

- Lamb leg with mint sauce

Vegetables

- Goose fat roast potatoes
- Carrot swede mash

- Cauliflower Broc cheese

Extras

- Sage and Onion stuffing balls
- Yorkshire puddings

To Serve

- Gravy

Instructions:

1. Heat the oven to 180C.
2. Pop in your meat and cook, as instructed, 1 hour and five minutes for the lamb.
3. Place the caulis Broc cheese first, the roast potato next for 35 minutes, the stuffing balls after 25 minutes, and then Yorkshire puddings.
4. Microwave the frozen carrot swede smash.
5. As per packet instructions, let the gravy continue.
6. Have a note of when you intend to eat and go out, and remember how long it takes each part to go into the oven and where it has to go.
7. In the sauce, a little splash of red wine will make it taste handmade.

4.16 Fruity Cakes

Cooking Time: 30 minutes

Serving Size: 12

Ingredients:

- 1 teaspoon baking powder

- Large handful blueberries
- 300g self-rising flour
- 140ml milk
- 100g caster sugar
- 2 large eggs
- 100g butter

Instructions:

1. In a muffin pan, heat oven 180 and pop-paper baking cases.
2. Mix ambient temperature butter and sugars until well combined, then one at the moment, add an egg.
3. Incorporate flour and baking powder.
4. When combined, add the milk in gradually while introducing blueberries.
5. Blend pop into cake lining.
6. Bake until well rose and crispy, for 15-20 minutes.
7. Cool for ten minutes in a tray before the withdrawal.
8. Place a little water (or lime juice) with a few teaspoons of powdered sugar and sprinkle.
9. Drizzle the runny paste over the chilled, fruity cakes.

4.16 Bangers And Cheesy Mustard Mash

Cooking Time: 45 minutes

Ingredients:

- 3 red onions (sliced)
- Gravy
- 8-10 sausages
- 1 knob of butter
- 1 tablespoon oil
- 1 packet of grated cheddar cheese
- 1 packet of mash

To Serve

- 1 bowl of peas

Instructions:

1. Heat the oven to 180C.
2. Cook the sausages for 30 minutes in the oven.
3. Fry the sliced spring onions until tender, around ten minutes, in a little oil.
4. In the meantime, according to the guidance, microwave mash for five minutes.
5. Then add a bit of butter and melted butter.
6. Shake for a further thirty seconds and heat so that the cheese melts.
7. Create gravy with hot water, remove the onions from the heat, and add gravy into the combination of onions and whisk thoroughly.
8. In the oven, roast your peas. Offer with the sausages, scramble, and plenty of caramelized onions alongside.

4.17 Chicken Pesto Tart

Cooking Time: 30 minutes

Serving Size: 4

Ingredients:

- Large handful mozzarella
- A handful of cherry tomatoes
- 1 block of puff pastry
- Jar of pesto Russo
- ½ packet of chicken strips

To Serve

- Salad
- Butter
- Baby Potatoes

Instructions:

1. Defrost the pastry overnight, as directed.
2. Remove from the refrigerator as per the directions before use.
3. Heat the oven to 180C.
4. Roll out the pie into a straight elongated and mark a 1.5-centimeter margin along the pie's edge using a paring blade.
5. This will create the borders of your tart.
6. Strangle the pesto, but leave the pesto in the square that you have created.
7. Shake over the strips of chicken.

8. Now add a couple of cherry tomatoes that are halved.

9. The next top has plenty of rubbed mozzarella.

10.   Bake until fried and boiling, or 25 minutes.

11.   Serve with a tray of fresh peas, butter on top, and a side dish.

12.   Drizzle with extra virgin olive oil for warmth and flavor just before baking.

4.18 Friday Night Kebabs

Cooking Time: 30 minutes

Serving Size: 4

Ingredients:

- Garlic sauce
- Chilli sauce
- 2 packets of meatballs
- Handful Romaine lettuce
- Iceland tomatoes
- Handful onions
- 4 Iceland pittas

Instructions:

1. Heat the oven to 180C.
2. Cook the meatballs for thirty minutes.

3. Value the edge of your pitta bread partly before baking, as this makes opening your pitta even smoother after baking it. Toast your Pitta gently.

4. By carefully pressing in a knife, wrench it open but make sure it remains intact.

5. Cover with one or two meatballs and lots of garlic, then add cabbage, tomato, onion, chili sauce, and jalapenos.

6. For a better and more natural version, use unsweetened yogurt with grated cloves instead of sauce.

Chapter 5: Traditional Vikings Recipes

5.1 Ballyvolane Gravadlax with Cucumber Pickle

Cooking Time: 30 minutes

Serving Size: 8

Ingredients:

- 2 tablespoon black pepper
- 4 tablespoon fresh dill
- 2 tablespoon of sea salt
- 2 tablespoon sugar
- 900g 2 sides of salmon

For the Dill Mustard Mayonnaise

- 1 tablespoon of dill
- Salt and pepper
- 1 large egg yolk
- ½ pint of sunflower oil
- 1tablespoon of wine vinegar
- 1 tablespoon of white sugar
- 2 tablespoons of French mustard

For the Cucumber Pickle

- 1 small shallot
- 3 tablespoon hot water
- 1 cucumber
- 1 tablespoon salt
- 1 small red chili
- 4 tablespoon caster sugar
- 4 tablespoon rice vinegar
-

Instructions:

1. Mix in the cinnamon, sugar, spice, and dill.
2. Place one side of the fish on the cling film and scatter it on the solution to ensure that it is covered uniformly.
3. Cover this prepared portion with salmon on the other hand.
4. In the cling film, seal all the fish well and chill in the fridge. Turn it on for four days. On day 5, it will be set.
5. Break the cucumber lengthwise in half.

6. Slice rather finely, ideally if you have one, using the thinnest configuration of a mandolin.

7. Incorporate the sugar, spice, vinegar, and warm water in a bowl until mixed, then add the cucumber, parsley, and red chili.

8. Move to individual serving containers and put before serving to refrigerate overnight.

9. In a mug, mix the yolk, mustard, and sugar slowly until mixed.

10. When the solution has emulsified, incorporate the oil drop at a time, then add the vinegar and dill. With salt and black pepper, spray.

5.2 Chopped Steak with Mushroom and Bacon Gravy

Cooking Time: 50 minutes

Serving Size: 4-6

Ingredients:

- 1 tablespoon thyme leaves

- Salt and fresh (cracked) pepper

- ½ Pound bacon mine was smoked

- ½ cup beef broth

- 1 tablespoon Worcestershire sauce

- 1 ½ pound beef ground sirloin

- ½ medium onion (chopped)

- 2 cloves garlic (smashed)

- ½ cup heavy cream
- 8 ounces cremini mushrooms
- ½ ounce package wild mushrooms

Instructions:

1. To a simmer, warm the cream and then insert the dried mushrooms.
2. Stir in cream to coat them, and then let sit for thirty minutes.
3. Cook the bacon and put on hand towels until crispy.
4. Give a moderate chop to the bacon, reserving 4 bits for your burger to edge.
5. Drain all but two tablespoons of oil from the pot and cook it again over medium-high flame. On both ends, brown the burgers nicely.
6. To the pan, transfer a stick of butter and a tablespoon of olive oil and sauté the fresh mushrooms, onion, and cloves for a few minutes until the onions are tender and the mushrooms begin to brown.
7. Add the broth to make sure all browned pieces from the pan are scraped off.
8. Insert the thyme, Worcestershire sauce, the mushrooms, and their cream to soak. Sprinkle with salt to taste.
9. Dip the sauce back into the burger, turn heat low, and cook till the burgers are finished.
10. Garnish each burger with a bacon slice and a few slices of mushroom.
11. Use boiling toasted potatoes to serve.

5.3 Lingonberry Jam

Cooking Time: 55 minutes

Serving Size: 7

Ingredients:

- 3½ cups Sugar
- 2.2 pounds Lingonberries

Instructions:

1. Rinse the lingonberries and pick some particulates out of them.

2. Place in the main cooking pot with clean lingonberries.

3. Add sugar and store over moderate to low heat.

4. Take it to a rolling boil. Decrease the heat and cook for at least 30 minutes or until finished. The jam would be transparent in color.

5. If the jam is set by dumping some on an ice-cold tray, and if it does not work, the jam is primed.

6. If it runs, continue to cook over medium heat for even more time and replicate the experiment until it no longer runs.

7. Then use a candy thermometer, 220°Fahrenheit, to decide whether it is set. Put some rum on the lids.

8. Load the hot lingonberry jam with the pots, seal well with the cover and turn the jars inside out to create a vacuum.

9. Store in a cool and dry position until refrigerated.

Cooking Time: 60 minutes

Serving Size: 8

Ingredients:

For the Meatballs

- 2 tablespoon breadcrumbs
- 1 teaspoon sea salt and black pepper
- 500g minced pork
- 2 eggs, lightly beaten
- 2 tablespoon plain flour
- ½ teaspoon nutmeg
- 1 small onion

For the Broth

- Sea salt and black pepper
- Small bunch of parsley
- 2 liters water
- 3 tablespoon plain flour
- 200g spelt grain
- 1 tablespoon of sea salt
- 3 apples
- 100g butter
- 3 bay leaves
- 600g celeriac
- 2 leeks
- 5 thyme sprigs

Instructions:

1. For all the other meatball components, combine the minced pork.

2. Load the water into a frying pan for the soup, insert the spice and herbs and bring it to a boil.

3. To turn the meat ball paste into balls, use a scoop to drop them into the boiling water and allow them to cook for fifteen minutes before they rise to the surface, implying that they are cooked.

4. Select them with a slotted spoon from the liquid and toss them aside. In a jug, strain 800ml of the broth.

5. Meanwhile, slice and cut the celeriac into 2 centimeters cubes.

6. Slice and drain the leeks properly. Break the apples into 1-cm-thick pieces.

7. In a big saucepan, heat the butter.

8. Add the flour and mix well, then add a little to the stored broth, stirring steadily until the sauce is creamy, without any chunks.

9. Insert the celeriac and leeks and leave to cook for 20 minutes.

10. Insert the meatballs and apple and steam until the meatballs are hot, about five minutes before the end of heating.

11. Meanwhile, in many cold-water shifts, rinse the spelt kernel.

12.   Cook for 15 minutes in salted boiling water, then rinse.

13.   Spray with the rosemary or chervil, eat with the spelt; prepare the meatball mixture to taste with salt and black pepper.

5.5 Kringle Recipe

Cooking Time: 110 minutes

Serving Size: 8

Ingredients:

For the Crust Layer

- ½ cup butter cold
- 2 tablespoons of ice water
- 1 cup all-purpose flour

For the Icing

- ½ teaspoon almond extract
- Sprinkles almonds
- 2 cups powdered sugar
- 1 tablespoon butter softened
- 4 tablespoons milk

For the Filling Layer

- 3 large eggs
- ½ teaspoon almond extract
- ½ cup butter (1 stick)
- 1 cup all-purpose flour
- 1 cup water

Instructions:

1. Heat the oven to 350°C. Line a baking tray or a silicone pad with baking parchment.

2. Break the butter into chunks. Combine the flour and cold bits of butter in a medium dish.

3. Cut into the pastry, using a blade or cookie cutter, until pea-sized crumbs develop.

4. Spray with ice water, then mix until a moist dough shape appears with a fork. Divide the dough into two separate parts.

5. Shape a thin strip for each part. Push on to the lined baking sheet using the back of a large beaker.

6. Combine the water and butter in a small saucepan; bring to the boil. Remove from the heat and stir in the flour instantly. Until clean, shake.

7. Add the eggs, one at the moment, whisking with each inclusion, until smooth. Integrate almond extract.

8. Split the stuffing from the crust side between the two crusts, stretching and piping up to ¾ -inch.

9. Bake for 50-70 minutes, until lightly browned and puffy.

10.   Take from the oven and cool absolutely for 1 hour at the very least.

11.   As the Kringle cools, the filled layer will shrink and slide.

12.   Combine the icing sugar, three tablespoons of milk, oil, and almond extract in a small bowl and stir.

13.   Add additional milk, one teaspoon at a time, until soft enough to sprinkle if the icing appears to be too dense.

14.   Drizzle the icing on each Kringle. If needed, top with sparkles or sliced almond.

5.6 Shaved Winter Vegetables Salad

Cooking Time: 40 minutes

Serving Size: 4

Ingredients:

- Balsamic glaze
- Salt and black pepper
- 1 small golden beet
- 4 lettuce leaves
- Olive oil
- 1 purple rainbow carrot
- 4 small radishes
- 1 small red beet
- 1 watermelon radish
- 1 orange carrot
- 1 black radish

Instructions:

1. Scrub the broad radishes and the beets; however, they do not clean.

2. On the ⅛ inch position of your mandolin, cut the leafy stalk end off and cut.

3. To get the pieces just right, this may require a bit of trial and mistake.

4. Place the slices on a clean plate and cover them as you work with a damp kitchen towel.

5. Slice and dice the carrots the very same way.

6. Put a sheet of dill or leaves or two broccolis on any of 4 side dishes to arrange your salads.

7. Begin with the larger rounds in a loose stack and arrange the vegetables.

8. Place the smaller carrots on top. Sprinkle with balsamic glaze and vegetable oil.

9. Spray with salt and black pepper gently and serve straight away.

5.7 Chocolate Cake

Cooking Time: 120 minutes

Serving Size: 1 cake

Ingredients:

- ½ teaspoon grated lemon zest
- Optional toppings
- 150g sticks butter
- 2 teaspoons vanilla sugar
- 150g white chocolate

- A pinch of salt
- 2 eggs
- 150g cake flour
- 200g granulated sugar
-

Instructions:

1. Heat the oven to 180°C, first of all.
2. Next, over reduced temperature, melt the butter in a frying pan.
3. Remove from the fire and stir the squares of white chocolate until they melt.
4. The egg and granulated sugar should be beaten together until light and fluffy.
5. Use a hand-held electronic whisk or a stand blender.
6. In a separate dish, combine the flour mixture and insert softly into the egg and sugar mixture.
7. Place in the chocolate-butter and lime zest until mixed.
8. Load into the cake pan ready. Put it directly in the oven and bake.
9. Bake until the cake is only under-baked for about 15-17 minutes.
10. The core should always be very moist because it should be cooked entirely on the side.
11. As baking times can vary, keep a close eye on it. It also wants a bit more time in the oven if it wobbles.

12.   Before moving to a serving tray, allow the cake to cool entirely in the pan for at least an hour.

13.   If you think you have overbaked it, quickly remove it from the tin to avoid the baking process.

5.8 Finnish Salmon Soup

Cooking Time: 20 minutes

Serving Size: 4

Ingredients:

- ¼ teaspoon allspice
- Salt and pepper to taste
- 1 lb. salmon filet
- 1 cup fresh dill
- 1 cup heavy cream
- 1 lb. Russet potatoes
- 1 large carrot
- 1 large leek
- 5 cups of water
- Four tablespoons unsalted butter

Instructions:

1. Strip the salmon from the skin and cut it into large chunks. Drop and discard all tiny pin bones.

2. In a soup pot, heat the butter and sauté the leeks for ten minutes or until they are nice and fluffy.

3. Add five cups of water and the preserved fish skin in a frying pan while the leeks are frying and bring to the boil, turn the heat down, and occasionally stir for ten minutes. You can miss this phase if you are using fish stock.

4. Strain the liquid and add the potatoes, vegetables, and half of the fresh dill to the skillet with the leeks.

5. Cook for ten more minutes, just until the potatoes are only fluffy.

6. Together with the cream and allspice, add the fish chunks to the broth and boil gently over low heat until heated through just a few other minutes.

7. Insert the leftover dill and, to satisfy, salt and black pepper.

5.9 Icelandic Pancakes

Cooking Time: 15 minutes

Serving Size: 24

Ingredients:

- ¾ cup margarine
- Milk, as required
- 2 cup flour
- 2 eggs
- 1-2 teaspoon cardamom
- 1 tablespoon sugar
- ⅛ teaspoon baking soda

Instructions:

1. In a pan, combine the flour mixture. Beat the eggs in a separate mixing dish.

2. Mix softened butter and an extract of cocoa.

3. To give a thick, thin mixture, continue adding the components together.

4. Then slowly add milk if needed, and mix to produce a batter of runny texture.

5. To let everything stabilize, let the batter set for 30 minutes.

6. Butter a pan and cook until the oil is fragrant over medium-high heat; add enough batter to cover the pan in a thin layer.

7. Enable it to cook until golden brown on the rim, then turn the small pancake over on the other side to brown.

8. It is essential that you need to spin the pan as you add the batter into the pan.

9. This makes the batter scatter across the surface finely and easily.

10. Flip it on a plate to dust with sugar and cinnamon, roll up tightly until baked, or stack it on a sheet to fold in whipped cream or fruit.

5.10 Midsummer Cocktail

Cooking Time: 10 minutes

Serving Size: 4

Ingredients:

- ¼ oz. St. Germaine elderflower liqueur
- Twist of lemon
- ¾ oz. manzanillo sherry
- 1 ½ oz. aquavit

Instructions:

1. In a mixing glass filled with ice, add all the ingredients and stir for 30-45 seconds.

2. Strain into a bottle of cooled coupe and season with a twist of citrus.

5.11 Rice Pudding with Marinated Oranges and Whipped Cream

Cooking Time: 65 minutes

Serving Size: 4-6

Ingredients:

Marinated Oranges

- 1-2 tablespoon dark rum
- 2-3 oranges
- 100ml water
- 2 cloves
- 2 cardamom pods
- 90 g granulated sugar

RI's À La Malta

- ½ teaspoon vanilla bean powder
- 1-2 tablespoon powdered sugar
- 1 cinnamon stick
- 150 ml of heavy cream
- 90g short-grain white rice
- ¼ teaspoon flaky salt
- 500 ml of milk

- 200 ml of water

Instructions:

1. In a frying pan, combine the water, sugar, spices, and cardamom seeds.

2. Cook it, then boil for 6-8 minutes, stirring now and then, till the syrup is caramelized slightly.

3. Remove from heat and add the rum, and stir. Now let it cool. To extract the peel and the white rind, cut the sides of the oranges away, then shave the sides back.

4. Cut the oranges finely and put them in a dish. Pour the syrup over the orange pieces, cover the dish, and leave to marinate for at least three hours in the fridge.

5. Before serving, remove the cloves and cardamom pods. In a frying pan, put the rice, salt, and water.

6. Let it simmer and cook with the cover on for ten minutes.

7. Insert the milk and cinnamon sticks and boil gently on medium heat with the cover on until caramelized, about 30-35 minutes, swirling now and then to ensure that it does not burn.

8. Take the cinnamon stick from the flame, discard it and let it cool slightly.

9. Along with the cocoa and sugar, whisk the cream to stiff peaks and then mix the whipped cream into the rice pudding.

10. With the citrus slices and sugar, serve the ris à la malta.

5.12 Smoked Mackerel with Horseradish Cream

Cooking Time: 10 minutes

Serving Size: 1

Ingredients:

- Dill a few fronds
- Salad to serve
- Radishes 5 (sliced)
- Rye bread 2 slices
- Mackerel 1 large fillet
- 2 tablespoon white wine vinegar
- 2 tablespoon soured cream
- 1 tablespoon horseradish sauce
- 1 teaspoon caster sugar

Instructions:

1. In a pan, place the radishes.
2. Combine the sugar and vinegar, season, and spill over the radishes. For ten minutes, leave.
3. Stir and spice the mixture and the horseradish. Over the rye bread, place.
4. Place the mackerel, the soaked radish, and a little dill on top. Serve with lettuce.

5.3 Rosemary and Thyme Roasted Rsdishes

Cooking Time: 40 minutes

Serving Size: 4

Ingredients:

- Pinch of salt
- Minced chives
- 2-3 whole radishes
- Sprinkle of thyme
- Sprinkle of rosemary
- Drizzle of extra virgin olive oil

Instructions:

1. Toss the radishes with a little extra virgin olive oil, rosemary, minced thyme, and a sprinkle of salt in a cookie sheet lined with parchment.

2. Roast for around 30 minutes in the oven at 350°F. Serve with clean chives.

Cooking Time: 60 to 120 minutes

Serving Size: 4-6

Ingredients:

- 300ml double cream
- 2–3 tablespoon breadcrumbs
- 2 125g tins Swedish anchovies
- 300ml full-fat milk
- 60g butter
- 1.25kg potatoes
- 2 teaspoon sea salt flakes
- black pepper
- 400g 2 large onions
-

Instructions:

1. Heat the oven to 200C
2. In a large frying dish, melt four tablespoons of melted butter.
3. Insert the onions, scatter with a half teaspoon of sea salt powder, and stir over moderate heat for a few minutes.
4. Turn down the heat until they begin to lose their raw appearance, and simmer very gently for 20 minutes.
5. Keep a close eye on them, and frequently stir: they are expected to be fluffy and pale yellow.

6. You should sprinkle a little more water into the skillet if they begin to stick or add more butter.

7. Use a flexible spatula to brush them and their buttery fluids into a bowl until they are ready.

8. In the buttered bowl, put a quarter of the potatoes. Sprinkle with salt and pepper.

9. Cover the potatoes with half of the soft onions, supplemented by a tin of sprouts.

10. The second quarter of the potatoes, salt, and black pepper, as before, was accompanied by the leftover onions and the third tin of sprouts.

11. Top it with potatoes for the backline. In a container, mix the milk and butter and spill it over the potatoes. It would not cover them.

12. Push down those that poke out, only so that the fluffy milk is thinly hidden, but do not panic if they come up again.

13. If using, scatter over the breadcrumbs and scatter over the leftover tablespoon of butter, then roast for 1 hour, but examine at 45 minutes: drive the fork in and cook the vegetables if it encounters no resistance.

14. They are gold on top, for sure, but they must be soft inside.

15. The gratin can stand until required for a bit and tastes almost as well, if not better, warm instead of steamed.

Conclusion

Combined with heavy emphasis on wellbeing and ethical developmental philosophy, the Nordic Cuisine platform has a creative approach to conventional foods. Nordic cuisine, nationally and globally, will build and encourage the pleasure of cooking, flavor, and variety. Nordic dishes are typically simple, and seafood, potatoes, meat, and berries being used in many traditional meals. Fresh, raw ingredients that can be found in abundance or that come freshly from the seas are the basis of most Nordic cuisine. Nordic cuisine has so much more to it than smoked salmon and meatballs. The Nordic food culture is much more complicated than you would imagine, ranging from Norway's midnight sun to the flat, green fields of Denmark. That said, many dishes and flavorings tie all the areas together, recreating a memorable experience of Nordic cuisine. Hundreds of years of heritage and common culture have created it and a bit of Viking plunder. Nordic cuisine is straightforward, and this is called husmanskost-the farmer's fare. It is normal and genuine, made with the land's staple product. There is no reason to over-complicate things when you deal with the very finest produce of Nordic cuisine. Consider trying at least some of these beautiful Nordic dishes from the book with easy and affordable recipes.

Printed in Great Britain
by Amazon

70549953R00068